I0154254

Lucinda Boyd

The Sorrows of Nancy

Vol. 1

Lucinda Boyd

The Sorrows of Nancy
Vol. 1

ISBN/EAN: 9783337778293

Printed in Europe, USA, Canada, Australia, Japan

Cover: Foto ©Thomas Meinert / pixelio.de

More available books at **www.hansebooks.com**

THE SORROWS

OF

N|A N C Y.

BY L. BOYD.

———————

RICHMOND, VA.:

O. E. FLANHART PRINTING COMPANY,

1899.

THE SORROWS OF NANCY.

BY L. BOYD.

History should be painted as a stern god-
dess, with Truth on her right hand and Memory on her left, while in the background should
appear tradition, like a wandering light,
glimmering along the quicksands of oblivion,
and in the foreground should stand an angel
pointing to the future.

A man's book is the visible sign of the invisible spirit that is in him. It is his brain-
child over which he yearns in love and pity. It
is an entity that may go down the ages and
live in the praises of men forever, or it may

be slain in the arena of public opinion. If the writer has told the truth and his book be thus cruelly slain, it will have a resurrection and come forth at last triumphant.

To write the truth concerning the birth and birth-place of Abraham Lincoln (so called) was suggested to me as follows:

I visited Washington, D. C., for the first time, about ten years ago. As I was approaching the Capitol I came in sight of the statue of Chief-Justice John Marshall, seated. There, thought I, is the finest likeness of President Lincoln I have ever seen. I looked at it for some time from all points of view before I read the name. After reading the inscription, a certain saying of my father's flashed across my mind, and I determined to learn the truth—*the whole truth*—concerning President Lincoln's ancestry. I have done so—as the following affidavits will show.

I believe that President Lincoln was a brave, good man. I believe also that the people of the North were the *only ones* who rejoiced at his death. The South knew, too well, that at his death her only friend had departed from the Council of those who held her destiny in the hollows of their hands.

Into the "Sorrows of Nancy" I have woven *facts,* traditions, and fancies. Should the story live, coming generations will do me justice; should it die, let it sleep with the pure motive that gave it birth—the love of *Truth!*   L. BOYD.

The Sorrows of Nancy.

In sight of the Blue Ridge mountains, in the " Old Dominion," stood a rude, log cabin, in the latter part of the last century. There lived in this cabin, at that time, a young woman named Lucy and her only child, Nancy. Nancy was a little child, and was to be pitied, for she had no legal right to her father's name, which was a high-sounding one, and had been coupled with honor for hundreds of years before she was born.

To say that Nancy lived in sight of the Blue Ridge Mountains is to say that she saw from her mother's cabin the " changing glories" that float along their misty tops at dawn and at eventide, and that she searched for wild flowers among the shadows of their deep valleys, and reflected through her whole after-life a part of the grandner she had absorbed among the scenes of her childhood, which would have refined and educated even an ordinary child, and Nancy was no ordinary child.

There was an old woman called Nancy, who lived with Lucy, and who was called Old Nancy to distinguish her from young Nancy. This woman had seen better days, and had received a fair education, for the times in which she lived. She was young Nancy's teacher in that solitary spot, and had taught her to read and write. For these accomplishments young Nancy had little use, as she possessed but one

book in the world—Bunyan's " Pilgrim's Pro-
gress "—and one friend outside of her
mother's cabin, to whom she did not need to
write, as she saw her daily.

This friend was a negress, who lived in a
hut not far away from her mother's door, and
took care of the cows and sheep that belonged
to her master.

If uneducated people have a fair average
of good, common sense, they are invariably
the best story tellers—because they draw their
metaphors and trophes from nature, and these
are always original and oftentimes sublime.

This negress was named Joult, and was
wise beyond her day and generation.

A cold spring evening was drawing to a
close on the scene around Lucy's cabin; while
on the mountain tops there gleamed a pale

electric light among the gathering shadows. Lucy chopped some wood, made a fire on the wide hearth of her cabin, and made some corn-meal mush—the only kind of food the family had tasted for weeks. Afterwards she took some rolls and began to spin on the big wheel. Old Nancy was carding rolls in the chimney corner. It is to be regretted that spinning (on the big wheel) has been discontinued, for no exercise could be more beneficial to the health, nor is any other half so graceful. The firelight was the only light in the room, and its fitful, flickering rays fell on Lucy's lythe form as it went back and forth to the whirr of the wheel. Her long hair, unbound, fell in waves far below her waist. The expression of her face was melancholy in the extreme, and added to the charm of her beauty.

There was a knock at the door. Little Nancy
ran to open it, and Joult walked in and sat
down in the corner opposite to old Nancy.
She did this with an air of condescension—for
she belonged to an aristocrat, a very rich man
in the neighborhood, and felt herself far above
the family she visited, and she was, certainly,
much better dressed than any member of it.
Little Nancy drew a stool to the side of Joult,
who had filled and lighted her pipe, and was
smoking in contemplative mood, and had said
nothing since her entrance, but " Good even'
to ye." Directly little Nancy looked in her
face and said: "Aunt Joult, what's your
soul?" Joult took her pipe from her mouth,
and, looking at Nancy with a puzzled expression on her jet-black face, replied: " Lord,
Gawd Amighty, chile, w'y hit's youah sper-

ret--you a great, big gal en kin read en write, doan know dat?" "Did you ever see one, Aunt Joult?" Joult thought a while before answering: "Yes, I did onct. I wur livin' right heah in dis heah cabin," pointing in the direction of her hut with her pipe, "en I done ben to a funel. Jess done die—po fellah—en I wur late gittin' home—en jes' es I git in de valley—at de foot ob de snail shell—I seed sumpen go 'bop' by me—en dah! bless Gawd, I see a hoss douten a head on 'im gwin by me lek de win'. My hoss wur dat scud dat he rared up—he rared up—en me specin' ebery minit fur to go clean ober his head. But I hilt on, do—en when I git home I doan git done trimblin de whole night." Little Nancy looked in the fire and seemed lost in thought. "Aunt Joult," said she, "will you be a horse when you die?" "A hoss! Listen at dat now! A hoss! Who say I gwine be a hoss? I not gwine talk long ob you ef you talk dat away. Ole Miss say—en she know—dat I gwine be white es she am when I dies." Old Nancy, to pacify her, said: "Tell us about the fort, Joult, Nancy is a child, and talks like one." "Dat too long," said Joult, "but ef you wan't me fur to tell hit, I kin." Lucy stopped the wheel. Old Nancy laid aside her cards, and little Nancy put her elbows on Joult's knee, and over all the firelight played with flickering, fitful blaze. The picture was one to which Rembrant could have done justice—as he of all the artists of the world knew how to paint shadows.

Old Joult began, after lighting her pipe: "When ole Moss come heah to settle, he lef' ole Miss in de settlemint at de Fort—en his niggahs, too—en he buy me en Jess on de way heah. So we come on, we did, wid ole Moss en a passel ob po' white men wha' he fotch along wid 'im fur to build his cabin— case we 'bleged fur to lib in a cabin till we git de big house built whut Ole Moss lib in now. Well, suh! when de cabin wur done—hit wur chunked wid stones en mud f'um top to bottom, en jis' little holes, fur light to come in, 'bout big es a man's head en bouten es high fum de flo'. Ole Moss, he hab de flo' ob de cabin built a considabul way fum de groun', en you 'bleged fur to go up steps fur to git in at de do'. I foun' out whut Ole Moss do dat fur atter while. We hab a cow en a hog or two, en chickens, en, suh! we hab a rooster whut could outcrow Ginil Washinton, an he crow *all de time*—hit 'peared to me, en rared 'roun' continaly, lek he wan' to fight. He cotch hit fur dat foolishtnest. Ef he done been a peacable roostah, he mought a ben livin' to-day. Oh, yes, we hab a dog, too, name Towser, en Ole Moss think de worle en all ob dat dog. He nevah mek no noise; he up en bites when de time comes. Well, suh! one evenin' a man come ridin' past Ole Moss's cabin wid his hoss all in a lathah ob sweat, en hollah to Ole Moss dat de Injuns wur a-comin'—dat dee done kill a whole pas-sel ob people, en wur a-comin' dis away, en dat he bettah mek his way to de settlemint— en den he rid on, he do, et de top ob his voice. Ole Moss, he look up at de sun, en say: " Hit am not more'n a hour high, en he not got time to mek de Fort, en he not gwine risk hit." He call all de men en Jess and me, en say: " Kill de hogs; tek up de flo', en kill right undah hit, so de Injuns cayn't see de blood, en drive de cow into de woods, en de hosses, drive dem, too, en kill de chickens en put em undah de flo', too, en Towser—poor Towser—I hab fur to kill Towser, or loss de life ob ebery man Jack ob us." I seed Jess look kinder quare, en I gib 'im a nudge. " Did they kill Towser, Aunt Joult, did—" " Now, hush, little Nancy, I gwine tell you treckly. You jes' listen. I's a-talkin' now." She paused and put a straw through the stem of her pipe, filled it leisurely, lighted it by putting a coal of fire on it, began to puff and resumed her story.

" De fust cotch de hogs, en tuck en knock 'em in de head en put 'em undah de flo' en cut de throats, en den me en Jess, we climb up de tree—case de chickens done gone to roost by dat time—kaze hit wur nurly dark. We tuck de chicken by de neck en choke 'em en den fling 'em down to Ole Moss en he cotch 'em. I cotch dat roostah. I do declar'—I wur right sorry fur 'im, so I wur, caze he fit lek a man en nuvah screech en squall lek de hens—he jes' fit en say nothin'. He lek to get away onct or twict. Ole Moss say, ' Joult, why'n you fling down de roostah?' I say, ' I's comin', Ole Moss.' So I helt de roostah twill I got to de las' limb ob de tree, en han' 'im to Ole Moss— kaze I not gwine kill 'im. I nevah kin furgit dat roostah, kaze he wur a purty thing en crow lek his wanpike done been mek outen brass, stridden meat, en stuff.

"Den Jess he turn to Ole Moss en say: ' Ole Moss, sarvant, suh! I gwine tek de

hosses—ride one en lead t'other—en dribe de
cow a piece in de woods, en leab 'em, en take
Towser en go on, ef you gwine gib youah
cornsent—kaze Towser he am nurdly people,
anyhow, en I cayrn't kill 'im, Ole Moss; *endeed
I cayrn't.'*   Ole Moss's eyes farly wartered
when he say, ' Gawd be wid you, Jess, you kin
go.' So Jess he cotch de hosses en druv de
cow off a piece, en Towser he galloped along
lek he done been tried fur 'is life en jes' gut
loose. We'uns all got undah de flo' en lay
down. De men kick up sich a dust a gittin'
undah de flo' an' a puttin' down de punchins
afterwurds dat I up en sneeze—en, suh! Ole
Moss he gimme such a plot in de side dat I
tuck a stitch in hit—en dah I wur, en feared
to hollah! Way long in de night we hearn 'em
comin'. Dee kick up a powful hellabolu, but

no dog bark, no hen cackle, no hog grunt; but way off in de woods Specklefoot she bawl lek she wan me fur to come to 'er. De Injuns come up to de house en clim' up en look in de holes; all wur dark en de cayrn't see nuffin. I wur feared de mought hear my heart a-beatin'—kaze I hean hit my own sef—bip, bip, bipetee-bip—en I wur afeared to draw my breaf. Treckly de yallah dogs busts de do' wide open en walk right squa' acrost wha' I wur a-layin'. Den de struck a flint—we hearn 'em—en I say to myself, 'We'uns done clean gone—dee'll git us now.' But, no, suh, he tar 'roun' en hollah lek de gwine bust deeselves, en den de went off jes' es dee come. We nevah crawl outen dat place till broad daylight, en den we crope out, en Ole Moss tuck us to de settlemint. Dat's wha' I seed dat

awful snake. I gwine home now. I gwine tell
you 'bout dat, little Nancy, anuddah night.
Tell you whut! Ef little Nancy tek de right
cayre ob herself, she gwine be a beauty. Dat
she am."

There was a rocky bridle path just at the
foot of the hill on which Lucy's cabin stood,
and close to the path that led down to it grew
a spreading beech-tree. In this tree Nancy
had watched a pair of robins build their nest
for three successive springs. The nest was
finished now, Nancy knew, and the mother
bird sitting on it, for Cockrobin sang to her
morning and evening, and filled the air with
the melody of love. And, what time he was
not foraging for dainties to regale her appe-
tite withal, he strutted in the sunshine on the
bare trunk of a fallen tree. Nancy loved to

watch him. The little mite was filled with pride; he was soon to be a father; he would hand down his name to future generations. At that thought he hopped along a few steps, and then stood straight up and looked like a fat man with his hands in his pockets strutting the streets of some great city thinking: " I have filled my barns. I have builded houses; my children are coming on, and I shall never want." Cockrobin snatched a worm that crawled before him and flew to his mate, and while she devoured it he sang his loudest notes. If he had only known what was before him, they would have been notes of farewell. He flew back to the log, and began to strut, as before. On the mountain side, bathed in the light of early morning, was the Judas-tree. She flaunted her beautiful dress in the face of

other trees less grandly clad, as if to say:
" Look at me! I am the loveliest tree in the
forest, and I have lovers whose names are
countless." An old tree, clothed in grave,
dark green, whose branches towered above
the Judas-tree in mighty strength, seemed to
shake its head at her, and say: " Your beauty
is short-lived. I shall be here when the places
that know you now shall know you no more
forever; for mine is the beauty of strength."
The young trees in their pale-green garniture
laughed back at the Judas-tree—as if they
knew a thing or two—while below the wild
flowers and the sweet Anemone kept their
own counsel. Cockrobin's time had come.
Never more; oh, never more! should he fly
from the Sunny South and build his nest in the
shelter of the Blue Ridge, nor lead his young

in its shadowy valleys, nor cleave the air of their misty tops, for the sharp crack of a rifle was heard, and he lay weltering in his blood. Nancy uttered no cry. She ran to where he lay when he fell from the tree trunk and took him to her bosom, and his life-blood flowed above a heart tender and true in its love for him. Her silent tears fell fast. A boy about fifteen came out of the thicket at the foot of the mountains and walked swiftly to Nancy's side. Her beauty kept him silent a moment, and then he said, with a deprecating look, " I did not know you were here or I should not have killed the bird. There are thousands about here. I will catch you a young one, and you can put it in a cage." " No," said Nancy, " another bird wouldn't feed his mate in that tree," pointing to the beech with her blood-

stained hand. " She'll die; I know she will."
And she wept afresh. Death and life are
mysteries to a child, and death is a hopeless,
awful mystery. A child, as well as his elders,
perceives, when he is brought in contact with
his icy breath, that gone never to return is
written on all things that he touches with his
invisible hand, and while his grief is of short
duration, its unreasoning depths know no consolation. At length the boy said cheerfully:
"Come! let us bury Cockrobin with the honors
of war." Nancy was so much awed by the
dress and manner of the boy that she laid her
dead friend in his outstretched hand and followed him to the foot of the beech-tree without a word. There the boy hollowed a little
grave and laid the dead bird in it and covered
him over. Such a little, little grave as it was,

and only the grave of a little bird, for whom
there was no resurrection (?), and who was not
allowed to live out the span of life *his* Father,
the Infinite One, had vouchsafed to him here.
The boy turned to Nancy, saying, " Don't cry,
little girl; I am sorry." Children understand
one another readily, and are good judges of
human nature. Nancy knew that the boy
was sorry for what he had done, but she could
not forgive him just yet. " What is your
name, and where do you live? " " My name is
Nancy, and I live in the cabin on the hill."
" My name is Andrew," said the boy, at part-
ing. They went their different ways—*they
who were to influence one of the greatest nations
of the earth.*

Nancy went to Joult's cabin and found
her smoking in her doorway, and wept as she

poured out her griefs to her. Her intuitions were unerring. Joult was full of sympathy for her, and, after puffing a while, she began the task of consolation.

" Lemme tell you, Nancy, dat robin you's so sorry fur gwine git annuddah mate fore long, lessen she's not lek people. Whut do she know 'bout deaf, en whut do she kuah? Why yistiddy I sot right heah in dis heah do' en I seed sumpen dat sot me a-thinkin'. You sees dat rail yondah? Well, suh! yistiddy mawnin' a po' worm wur a humpin' hissef along on dat dah rail en a doin' fur hissef, en along come Mistew Robin a doin' fur hissef, too. He see dat worm en dat worm see him, en knowin' whut he wur attah he fall offen dat rail en hide hissef undah hit, en Mistew Robin he fly off—he do. Treckly de worm say to hissef, 'De robin done gone, now I gwine home.' He crawl out—he do—en gun fur to mek his way crost de log—when down come Mistew Robin en snatch him ball headed in a minnit. He tuck 'im—he do—en he roll 'im in de dus'—he roll 'im in de dus'—jes' lek Ole Moss hab de niggahs do de hogs in de hot wattah when dee done dead en cayan't holp deeselves." Joult puffed and puffed, and Nancy, thinking that she had finished, rose to go, when Joult resumed: " Yes, indeed, honey, people's mean en robins am mean, when he gits a chance. I boun' some ole robin done been a skylarkin' 'bout dat widdah long befo' dis, chile."

That night Joult did not make her appearance at Lucy's cabin, and little Nancy retired early. It was her birthday, but she did not

know it. It had always been a day of mourn-
ing with Lucy as often as its anniversary came
around. She did not spin that night, but sat
before the dying fire, and grieved in silence.
Old Nancy replenished the fire and sat down
near Lucy, and put her hand on her bowed
head and said kindly: " Lucy, tell your story;
it will do you good. Tell it, Lucy, now that
little Nancy is asleep; it will ease your mind.
" There is little to tell. You know, Nancy,
that the best blood of Virginia runs in little
Nancy's veins, but that doesn't comfort me. I
want her to know, when I am dead, and that
will be before long, that I fell through my affections, and that I have suffered enough since
that time to atone for the sins of the whole
world. You know that Mr. M—— was handsome, and far above me in station, and he

used all the arts he was master of to entice
me from the path of right. But, oh, Nancy,
he loved me—indeed he did—and I loved him.
I should have been as willing to die for him
as Christ was to die for the sins of the world,
and God knows it. I proved it, for I became a
living sacrifice for his sake and suffer more
every day than if I died. The night before
he went away he came here; he made the
sweetest music on the bugle that was ever
heard. It echoed among the valleys as if it
came from Heaven and the angels were calling
the dead—the sainted dead, Nancy—only they
shall hear the angels at the last. He came in
and took little Nancy in his arms and kissed
her, and traced his own likeness in her features. He was tender and kind; and, oh,
Nancy, I could not reproach him. I loved

him, but I stood in awe of him as well, and that made me love him all the better—I believe. When he told me good-bye, he said: ' I am going to the frontier, Lucy, to meet danger, and it may be death: if I live I shall come back and marry you and take you across the ocean, and there we shall educate little Nancy and be happy. If I fall and fill a soldier's grave, my fate will be better than I deserve for my treatment of you. Should I survive and return, you shall hear my bugle sound among the mountains long before you see me. Dead or alive, I *will* come back to you, and the notes of the bugle shall call you to come to me, wherever I shall be!''

" And, Nancy, I never saw him again; but I have heard his bugle blowing and the sound dying away in a solemn wail among the valleys of the Blue Ridge often and often, when you were asleep, and it seemed to call me."

It was apparent to old Nancy that night, for the first time, that Lucy was failing, and that the end was drawing near.

All the poetry little Nancy had ever read was written in the scenery about her mother's cabin. The mornings that broke calm and still in springtime over the tall peaks of the Blue Ridge, and the lands that lay below them were, to her, Idyls of Youth and Love. The young trees were her friends and the old ones were her counselors. Those that lay dead taught her a lesson of death that was not repulsive. The summer, with its burning sun and noontide brightness, told her of the prime of life, and the burden and heat of the

day that came with mature years. Autumn
sighed of life's decline and of a beauty which
was fading, and had put on gorgeous colors to
hide the ravages of time. Winter, cold and
cheerless, to her, was an old man standing on
the borders of a rushing river, whose dark and
turbid waters, only, divided him from a
Better Land.

And what in all that world of grandeur
spoke to Nancy of Immortality? Not the flower
that dropped its seed and died. No. Another
plant of its kind came, but not the same one.
Gone *never to return* was written above its
grave. She had often and often watched a
worm make its own coffin; but she did not
know that the worm lay down in it, sure of a
resurrection. Another, wiser than she, taught
her that long afterwards.

One evening in the early fall old and young Nancy and Lucy sat under the beech-tree that was near the bridle-path at the foot of the hill. A grand gentleman, such as Nancy had never seen before, accompanied by Andrew, the boy who had killed the robin, rode up to where they were sitting and stopped. Andrew asked to be directed to the spring, as he wanted some water. Little Nancy's eyes were fixed on the old gentleman. His long hair was caught at the back of his head with a ribbon, and he was dressed in Continental style—that grand old fashion that made a common man look like a gentleman, and a gentleman look like a hero. He had on gold knee buckles, and his shoes were adorned with the same precious metal. How long little Nancy would have stood there taking in every detail of the old man's dress and features is not known. Andrew touched her, and she roused herself, and led the way to the spring.

While the children were gone, the old gentleman said to Lucy: " Whose child is that, Madame? " " Mine," said Lucy. " Who was her father? " said the old gentleman, fixing Lucy with his piercing black eyes. Lucy covered her worn face with her hands, and all the parts of her face and neck that were visible were covered by a deep blush. Nancy and Andrew soon returned. Andrew carrying a bucket of water with a white gourd in it, having a long handle—the only thing Lucy possessed to serve water in. Andrew handed the old gentleman a gourdful of water; he held it in his hand and stared at little Nancy. What could have moved him so? Nancy's face was

beautiful, but in looking at it the grand gentleman lost his self-control, and dashed the
gourd to pieces on the rocky bridle-path below, and rode away. Andrew gave little
Nancy a pitying look, and then mounted his
horse and followed his father. " Who is that,
Aunt Nancy? " asked little Nancy. Old
Nancy might have said truly, " That is your
grandfather "; but she said simply, " Judge
Chief-Justice M——." " Is Andrew his son? "
continued little Nancy. " No, he is the son
of his adoption, and not of kin at all. He is
the son of an Englishman, who came here and
died, and Judge M—— made him his heir
at law after his own son was killed on the
frontier, some years ago."

Lucy rose and tottered, as she walked
slowly to the cabin. She had a distressing

cough, and was growing weaker and thinner
day by day. When the leaves began to fall she
grew rapidly worse. She had let go the anchor
of life and was drifting away. It was soon apparent, even to little Nancy, that Lucy was
very ill, and Lucy knew and rejoiced that she
was soon to make her last earthly atonement
for the sin of her youth. Old Nancy and Joult
prepared such simples as they had been taught
were remedies for consumption, but they failed
to relieve the sufferer. Little Nancy was
thoughtful beyond her years, as solitary children always are. She had learned many les-
sons from mother Nature, but nothing had
taught her to face *her* mother's death. She
could not bear to contemplate such a calamity
as her loss.

The great events of this life are solitary.

Every human being comes from the shore of a past eternity alone, passes through Time—a stranger in a strange land—goes alone and without his volition into a future eternity, and there none but the dead may follow him.

The grief one feels for the dead must be borne alone; unaided one must conquer it, or it must conquer him, and no man may help him. None can win honor for another and none can lead a blameless life, except for himself. The good deeds of one's ancestors may reflect honor upon a man; but, if he would really possess honor, *he must win it for himself*. It took the Son of God to atone for the sins of the world, and He suffered death alone.

Poor little Nancy! She had but three friends in the world, and now she was about to lose the best one of them. Out of her mother's presence she wept bitter tears.

Her dying mother lay on her hard, straw bed awaiting the solemn change she knew must come, and her one thought was Nancy. "Oh, little Nancy! What will become of little Nancy?" Her sufferings were intense. Her bones wore through their covering, and her body was ready for the grave, while her soul retained its healthful vigor. "These vile bodies!" How they serve the souls that inhabit them! They often and often shut them up in silence and darkness—eye and ear refusing to do their office—and the poor soul, in its watchtower of clay, is unable to signal to those about it, and is glad to go to the deeper darkness and longer silence of the grave, even if the grave should mean everlasting sleep.

The anniversary of the Christ child's birth brought release to Lucy. She said to old Nancy on Christmas-Eve, " Stay with me to-night, Nancy, I shall be at rest in the morning."

The moon shone high in the heavens, and about midnight Lucy asked Joult to open the door. A long track of moonlight crossed the floor and touched the dying woman's face. She lifted her wasted arms, as if embracing some one, and her face was radiant with love, and so her soul passed—unseen by mortal eyes—into the immensity of space. Just as she died, old Nancy and little Nancy and Joult heard the sound of a bugle dying away among the dark valleys of the Blue Ridge.

Lucy was buried under the shade of the beech-tree. Slaves made her grave, and the rude coffin in which her body lay. They placed the clods of the valley above the wreck of what had once been a beautiful, innocent girl, and they did it reverently and tenderly. There was no minister to read at the grave of this poor outcast this most sublime passage ever written:

" I am the resurrection and the life, saith the Lord: he that believeth in Me, though he were dead, yet shall he live; and *whosoever liveth and believeth in me shall never die.*"

The dome of Heaven was her mausoleum and above her grave was whispered: " I am the resurrection and the life." and the winds answered *Resurgam.*

Through the winter that followed Lucy's death old Nancy and little Nancy barely lived. Joult divided her scanty store with them, and

Lucy's Grave.

in every way acted the part of a Christian to
these poverty-stricken tenants of the wayside
cabin. But the wolf howled at their door, day
and night, and they were often brought face
to face with that gaunt visitant, and alone they
could not have driven him away.

Spring came early that year, and was
unusually bright and warm. The mate of the
" Widder Robin " built his nest in the beech-
tree and sang as of yore, but his notes were a
dirge to Nancy, for he sang above her
mother's grave.

As the season advanced and the wild
flowers bloomed, Nancy took the brush that
had been piled above her mother's resting-
place to prevent the stock from trampling it,
and planted flowers about it, and built a rude
fence around it, and knelt reverently there to

pray, morning and night. The lights that
guided this daughter of the wilderness were
dim, but the All-Seeing eyes beheld her. Her
greatest trouble was that she could not sepa-
rate her mother's soul from her body—her
reason refused to do it, and her grief had in it
a tinge of despair.

Joult came down to Lucy's grave one
evening, when Nancy was weeping by it and
sat down beside her to offer consolation.

" Nancy," said she, " youah mamy's grave
look monstus purty sence you done put de
flowers on hit. En I tell you whut! she gwine
sleep jes' es well right dah—undah dat tree—
es ef she hab a great big mountment on 'er—
en she gwine hear Gable when he blow jis es
well en git out betteh den ef de stones hattah fly when she wake up. I feels fur you,
honey, I rally does, chile."

PART II.

How old Nancy and little Nancy came to
Kentucky, and with whom is not known.
Certain it is, however, that in the year 18—
they were living, with other women, in a cabin
on the line that divides Clark county from
Bourbon. After living in sight of the Blue
Ridge, no scenery would ever be complete to
Nancy without mountains in the distance.
Standing in the cabin door, she might see as
fair a prospect as the earth holds—rolling
meadow lands, covered with the richest blue
grass, shaded by trees of oak, maple, beech,
and elm that had taken centuries to mature,
and along Strode's Creek towered, then, as

now, the giant sycamore.   There were no farm
houses in the near vista, but on the air
was borne the hum of the water-mill,
whose wheel the waters of Strode's Creek
turn from sunup till sundown.   It is built of
stone, and its quaint structure adorned, and
still adorns, a scene of surpassing loveliness.
This mill was named Thatcher's Mill in honor
of its builder and owner.

If Strode's Creek—often Strode's River—
could speak, it could throw light upon a certain story that will now always remain a
mystery.   But it does not speak: it murmurs—
murmurs through the pleasant lands, as it had
done hundreds and hundreds of years before
the white man appeared on its banks to plant
the standards of civilization and freedom.   It
murmurs and complains and runs its way to

meet other streams that flow onward to the sea, and are swallowed up in the greater mysteries of its unfathomable depths that shall keep their secrets till the sea and the grave give up their dead.

One morning in October of the year 18— the winds were shrill and rustled the leaves as if they were tired of their clinging to their friends, the trees, and making a pretence of living, and sent them whirling and eddying to the ground, as if they bade them get into their graves and make way for the new, young kings of spring that were soon to reign in their stead.

Old Nancy helped little Nancy with a bundle of soiled clothes and a great iron kettle down to Strode's Creek, near the mill. Old Nancy, it was apparent, was getting infirm,

and her devotion to little Nancy seemed the
one link that still bound her to life. The old
woman put a stone under each leg of the
kettle, and, while little Nancy was gone to the
cabin for live coals to start a fire under it, she
filled it with water from the creek. Young
Nancy started the fire, drew her lythe form
to its full height, and looked to the East, and
the scene before her faded away, and in its
stead the cabin on the mountain side was
before her, and the mists of a spring morning
were rolling away from the distant peaks of
the Blue Ridge. She could see her mother's
grave and could hear the birds sing as she
had heard them in spring times long past.
Old Nancy regarded her with doting fondness,
then approached her, and took her in her em-
brace, saying: " You look like your poor

mother, Nancy, but more like your father to-day than I ever saw you look before. Something's going to happen." Old Nancy hobbled off to the cabin, and young Nancy stood where she had left her, still with her face in the direction of Virginia, and thinking of her mother's grave at the foot of the mountains. When the fire began to crackle and burn, it seemed to recall Nancy to a sense of her duty, and the day's work before her, and she took up a bucket and went to Strode's Creek. As she stooped over the stream, her brown, curling hair fell down and swept the water, and in that attitude she was struck motionless with her eyes fixed on an upper window of Thatcher's Mill. She had heard Andrew's voice, and knew it after years of separation. She listened, and, without filling her bucket, she rose to flee. As she stood up, Andrew's face appeared at the window. Nancy's dress was ragged and worn, but Andrew knew the fair face and form, that nothing, not even death, could disguise from his recognition, and he was beside her in a moment, had clasped her hand, and looked into her eyes with something very like love, and with unmistakable admiration in his own dark eyes.

The guardian angel of the outcast is tardy in his duty, and often forgetful of it entirely. Death is the only thing in the universe that is as strong as love. Why did he not do battle for Nancy on that fatal day, when she met Andrew, and claim her for his own, and save her from what followed?

Nothing in the slumberous air of that October day warned Nancy. She did as

women have ever done, since the beginning
of time—loved her affinity, no matter in what
station she found him.

Washington Irving says: "A woman's
whole life is a history of the affections." If
that be a woman's life, what is a man's? Is the
first half of it a history of unbridled passion,
and the last half a record of unavailing regret
and remorse?

If life were not such a serious puzzle, it
would be enough to make one smile to read
the discussions between man and woman as
to the superiority of the mental powers in man
to those in woman. Men and women, intel-
lectually, are not alike, and, therefore, may
not be compared; as things dissimilar differ,
not in degree, but in kind. A man has reason,
which is the power that enables him to ratioci-

nate: a woman has intuition, that stands side
by side with inspiration. A man toils to a
conclusion, and when he gets there, he can
point out step by step the road he came, and
prides himself on the mental strength he has
wasted and the way he has marked with his
blood-stained footprints. He exults over
woman, because he is stronger than she, and
because he has traveled where she can never
follow. Has he? Has he really walked where
she can never tread? Yes—when he hews and
builds and exerts his physical strength, only.
But the empire of mind is woman's sphere. A
woman's mind flies to a conclusion, and the
path by which she arrives at it is like the way
of a bird in the trackless air that is lost forever, but her deductions are as infallible as
man's. Man, with his attribute of reason, and

woman, with her swift intuitions, when joined together, *after being drawn together by mutual affinity*, make a complete spiritual circle, as God intended they should do, and each is the complement of the other, neither the superior.

Nancy washed the clothes and hung them to dry on the bushes; then went to a spring, which has since been called " Nancy's Well," and sat down to rest, leaning against a tree. She was never able in after life to tell whether she cognized what appeared to her with her waking or her sleeping vision.

She was thinking of Andrew, and of how handsome he looked as he rode away to Winchester, and smiled as she remembered his earnest promise to return, when all at once there shown out of the shadows of twilight, that were gathering, the face of a man. The face looked like Andrew's, but not so striking as his, except in expression. The eyes were tender and infinitely sad and prophetic. Then she saw, or thought she saw, a sea of human faces, all turned one way, and the man lay dead, his loving eyes closed forever by the hand of an assassin.

At that time, Winchester and Clark county were infants in their swadling clothes, but they were being trained and educated in the way they should go by Robert Elkin and the Traveling Baptist Church. How few men, in this world, have literally gone about doing good as did Robert Elkin—who rests now forever from his labors. His grave is in an open field, and soon the traces of it will be lost.

One night late in this same fall there was preaching at Thatcher's Mill, and the old divine, Robert Elkin, conducted the services. A preacher, in that early day, always drew large, if not attentive, audiences. There were no places of amusement in Clark county at that time, and men and women flocked to every place that promised excitement or recreation. Since civilization has spread its wings over Clark county the young citizens and citizenesses still long after the diversion which change of place may bring, and a party of young people will pay large sums of money to get away from civilized life and to play the savage in tents—make-believe wigwams— on the Kanawha River, in Virginia—proving, clearly, that a streak of savage blood still lingers in the veins of all the children of men.

Robert Elkin's text that night was this sentence: " Christ was a man of sorrows and acquainted with grief." The truths of the Gospel of peace on earth and good will to man are not perceived by the same vision that takes in the material things of this life. Intuition is the eyes of the soul, and faith is purely subjective. Robert Elkin's spiritual eyes had been opened. He had never heard of Confucius, who taught a religion similar to the Christian religion, five hundred years before Christ was born—" The Light of Asia " was nothing to him. He told the simple story of Christ's birth, life, death, and resurrection, and the people were moved to tears. Nancy heard him and wept for joy—that she should see her mother again. Andrew was there, but his spiritual eyes were closed, that he

might not see. When the sermon was done,
and a stirring song began, in which the whole
congregation united in singing, an old negro
woman rose up in a corner of the mill, clap-
ped her hands, and cried in a loud voice:
" Gawd bless the whole world." Then Nancy
saw Joult, the friend and comforter of her
childhood.

When the people began to disperse, some
one took a candle to light the preacher to his
horse, and Joult saw and recognized Andrew
hiding in the shadow of the mill, as if waiting
for some one. She paused to watch him.
When the people were all gone, she saw him
leave his hiding place, and swiftly follow
Nancy.

"Dah, now!" said Joult, "look at dat
snake in de grass. I gwine 'prove Nancy
when I sees her—dat I is."

The next morning little Nancy found Joult and after greetings were over, Joult sat down and began to talk: " Yes, indeed, honey, I git along monstus poly attah Ole Moss die. I hattah be sole, long ob de yuttah niggahs, en den de man whut buy de cows en sheep whut I tuck kure ob—he lef me in de cabin by my lone lorn sef—dout es much es a cat er a dog fuh to keep me comply. Peared to me when de night ud come down on de Blue Ridge dat de whole worle wur open befo' me. I do declah, when de win' chase de mist up en down de valley, hit look lek de dead done got outen de graves en come to judgemint. Youah mamy's grave wur a heap ob company fur me, too. De las' time I seed hit wur in de fall—befo' I came to Kaintuck—en hit wur covered wid leaves red en

brown en gole; de sun wur goin' down behind
de mountains en peared fur to kiss whur de
po' gal slep. But, Nancy, I gwine tell you: I
seed dat Ander a sneakin' en a hidin' roun' de
mill las' night till attah de people all git away,
en den tek out attah you. You mine whut I
tells you bouten a nasty, brute beas' ob a man
wha' am feared en shamed fur to be long ob
a gal 'fore uddah folks. 'Omen folks—more
obspecially."

*   *   *   *   *   *   *   *

Inlow, the miller, and Andrew sat under a
tree not far from the mill, on a fallen log, and
whittled sticks and meditated, while all about
them floated the incense of spring, and in the
tree-tops the birds sang fragments from the
Oratorio of the Resurrection.

Inlow had something on his mind; but, as

he looked at the young patrician beside him, he hesitated to make his thoughts an entity by embodying them in words. He sat in silence and, unconsciously, perhaps, shaped the stick he was cutting into a dagger, and, holding it up before Andrew, said: " If this wood were steel, you had better plunge it into Nancy's heart than stay here longer; if your intention is not to marry her. She loves you, and is beneath you. I hope that you are a man of honor." Andrew gave Inlow a searching look, and continued the use of his knife, in silence.

Why did Andrew linger in Kentucky? He rode past the few cabins, that composed Winchester, and bright eyes were gladdened at sight of the gallant, handsome youth. Many of the first settlers of Winchester were

educated, refined people, and Andrew enjoyed
their society; but, if Winchester had been
wiped out of existence, what then? He would
still have lingered around Thatcher's Mill, as
he had done for months.

Young men are not wicked *au fond;* they
seldom, however, do more than skim over the
surface of their motives—seldom or never
dive to their depths to learn if truth be at the
bottom.

Andrew rose at length, and walked in the
opposite direction to Nancy's cabin, and sat
down. He could hear his horse pawing the
ground under the tree to which he had hitched
him; he could hear the doves coo, coo, as they
built their nests—he was restless and unhappy.
He saw old Nancy and the women who lived
with her ride off in the direction of Win-

chester, and then did what he had often done before—went to the cabin, and found young Nancy sitting in the door looking in the direction of Virginia. As he sat down on the grass—not far from her—he thought that few young girls could bear the close inspection to which he subjected her as he sat there. She smiled and her teeth shone milk white; her cheek was dappled with red, like a ripe peach; but her hair was her glory—long, luxuriant, and of the richest brown.

Are there inherited traits - inate knowledge of the properties? Who shall say? Andrew, while looking at Nancy, said abruptly, watching the effect of his words: " I must return to Virginia soon." Nancy turned pale, and the light died in her dark eyes, but she struggled hard to keep the tears back and succeeded. Nancy had a proud old ancestress, whom she might not claim, from whom, perhaps, she had inherited self-control and unconquerable pride, for she said in a voice as indifferent as Andrew's own: " When do you leave? " " Soon," he replied, " my departure depends on the surveyors."

That man never lived who, if he heard a girl loved him, and were convinced of the fact before he heard it from another, did not seek the girl and prove it again and again, to the satisfaction of his own inordinate vanity. " *Vanitas vanitatis* " should be written above the story of every man's love—which is a mixture of passion and egotism. There *are many* very honorable exceptions, but the rest are a lot, and all named Abelard.

Nancy said, as if to change the subject, " I

should give half my life for one sight of the Blue Ridge. Is it memory that brings back the scenes I love so well before me in dreams? I seem to be there. I can *feel* the winds blow and hear the birds sing. Awake, I can shut my eyes and see the red-bud-tree and its taller friends bowing to one another as they used to do in spring times long passed." She paused and resumed, after a silence: " I shall never see the place again—not even my mother's grave." She wept bitterly. Did Nancy weep for a sight of her mother's grave? Andrew did not know, but he was determined to find out.

" Should you be glad to go to Virginia with me, Nancy? I am going soon; my business here is almost ended."

As Andrew said this, he watched her cheek

glow, and the light leap into her sad eyes. The blood of her haughty, old ancestors, that ran like fire in her veins, prompted her reply—" I do not understand you. *How should I go with you?*" The boy was abashed and puzzled by the proud look Nancy gave him, and he smiled to himself angrily as he thought: " *She* would hide her heart from me—even she—when I might have *any* girl for the asking."

A woman is braver than a man while excitement lasts, and could lead a forlorn hope or storm a citadel; but she could not beleaguer one—it takes a man to do that.

Andrew rose to go. " Good-bye, Nancy; I may not see you again." " Good-bye," said Nancy, simply, and then sat down in the doorway—unable to stand up or keep the tears back. At sight of Nancy's tears, Andrew reseated himself, took off his hat, pushed the black curls from his forehead, and smiled triumphantly. He was so rejoiced that he had gained a sure knowledge of Nancy's love for him that he told her that he loved her devotedly, and that she was beautiful, and sealed his statements with a kiss that was divine, Nancy thought, for it was the first kiss of her first love.

Late that evening Andrew came to the cabin again, and, finding the women returned, he proposed a walk with Nancy. They walked by Strode's Creek, that knows, but keeps its own secrets and sends them to their grave in the ocean. They sat long by " Nancy's Well "—so long that the moon made her image in the water to warn them that the hour was late. The owl wailed from

his solitary watch-tower in the distant wood,
and mourned to the spirit of darkness that all
was not well under the solemn stars. The
guardian angel of Nancy was fast asleep.

Weeks went by after this, and Andrew did
not return to Thatcher's Mill. Nancy went,
as in a dream, about the duties she was com-
pelled to perform, her whole being lost in the
yearning to see her lover once again. She
could bear the suspence his absence caused
no longer, and determined to go to Winchester. She persuaded old Nancy to borrow two
horses from Abraham Inlow, the miller, and
to accompany her.

Nancy dressed herself in a gown Joult had
given her, and which had belonged to Joult's
former mistress. It was made of fine material,
in a fashion long by passed; but it fitted her

slender form to perfection, and its dark folds brought out the rich tints of her beautiful complexion. Old Nancy brought out a bonnet of immense size—made of Leghorn, and yellow as gold from age. This bonnet was a relic from old Nancy's wardrobe in better days. Little Nancy put it on, and her young face looked all the prettier from its great depths. Dressed, she ran to " Nancy's Well," and as she saw her image in the pellucid water, she was surprised at the transformation fine clothes had wrought. As she stood by the spring, she might have been painted as the personification of beautiful youth. She should have been painted then, for she never looked like that again in all the world—her heart was broken that day.

Old Nancy and young Nancy hitched their

horses on the outskirts of the hamlet
of Winchester, and old Nancy sat down under
a tree to smoke, and young Nancy began
walking about the streets of the village, so
lately laid off and named. More than one man
looked, and turned to look again, at the beautiful face—radiant in the depths of that old
bonnet. Just as she passed the log courthouse she saw Andrew approaching her with
a lady on his arm—a *real lady*, as Nancy knew.
Andrew passed her without a word; but not
without a sign, for his face was as pale as
death would ever make it. " What lovely
barbarian is that? " Nancy heard the lady ask.
Andrew's answer was lost to her, but not the
meaning of his manner as he passed her. No;
it was as clear to her as it was to God. It
taught her that she was an alien, and an out-

cast forever from society. It whispered another truth to Nancy in two words, these— *fallen! forsaken!* Oh! angels of mercy, look down on this deluded girl.

When young Nancy returned to old Nancy and said: " Come; take me home; I am sick unto death," her white face—from which the light of youth had forever fled—confirmed her words.

Smile, if you will, you human beings of coarse nature, who do not believe that love— unrequited—as surely kills the sensitive girl, whom it wounds as the plowshare does the tender violet it upturns to the frosts of early spring.

Arrived at Thatcher's Mill, a young man— whom Nancy had never seen before—assisted her from her horse, and, although her face was white as marble, its beauty led him captive ever afterwards. Nancy saw and saw him not. She walked as one in a dream. Between her and all things of this life there was a handsome young face—pale as death and almost as cold and stern of expression. She hastened to the cabin, took to her bed, and lay there until midnight. When all were asleep, she stole to "Nancy's Well," and sat down by it, the image of despair—she who early that morning might have been painted as the personification of beautiful youth.

Two years went by, and all that time Nancy's new lover pressed his suit through Abraham Inlow. Nancy had ceased to live—only drifted with the tide of time. She consented to become the wife of Thomas Lincoln. They were not married in Clark county, but

in ———— ————. When they left Thatcher's Mill
to be married, there sat between them a child,
whose name was Abraham. He was a remark-
able-looking child, even at his tender age.
In after years his face had a rugged, melancholy grandeur, that once seen could never
be forgotten. His eyes had an expression
that was "infinitely sad and prophetic," as if
they looked on Death. Taken as a whole, his
face looked like the Sphinx, that might be an
image of death in its most sublime majesty—
waiting for all the generations of men to pass
before him, that he might wither them into
nothingness by a look.

Nancy died young, and her soul has long
since confronted the soul of the man, without
whom Abraham would never have been. She
died and was buried in Indiana. She was so

far honored above her mother—in her death—
that Robert Elkin read above her resting-
place this most sublime passage ever written.

" I am the resurrection and the life, saith
the Lord: he that believeth in me, though he
were dead, yet shall he live: and whosoever
liveth and believeth on Me shall never die."

Nancy Lived and Believed.

AFFIDAVITS.

The affiant, L. Boyd, states that a few days after the assassination of President Lincoln, her father, Rev. Samuel Rogers, born near Charlotte Courthouse, Va., in the year 1789 (a soldier in the war of 1812, and minister of the Christian Church in Kentucky and other States from the time, or shortly after the time, when Alexander Campbell founded the Disciples' Church, until 1877, when he died), said to her: " The grandmother of Abraham Lincoln was called by the several names of Lucy Hanks, Hornback, and Sparrow. Nancy, Lincoln's mother, was the child of Lucy Hanks, Hornback, or Sparrow and a son of Judge John Marshall, of

Virginia. Nancy Hanks, Hornback, or Sparrow was born near Lynchburg, Va., and in sight of the Blue Ridge Mountains, and at the foot of them her mother, Lucy, lies buried.

Nancy's father—son of Judge Marshall—was killed in " border warfare."

Lincoln's father was the adopted son (whether by law or not, I do not know) of the same Judge Marshall, of Virginia, mentioned above, and was the son of an Englishman, who fought and was killed in the same battle in which the said Nancy's father perished. Abraham (afterwards called Abraham Lincoln) was born near Thatcher's Mill, on or near the line that divides Clark county from Bourbon county, Ky., and was born out of wedlock. I have often seen the place where he was born.

Rev. Samuel Rogers is dead, as above stated, but in his life he knew Kentucky and Virginia well, and was among the first men who preached the new religion in those two States.

When I was called to Winchester, Ky., April, 1894, to write the history of Winchester and Clark county, the present ——— of Winchester, Ky., John ——. ———, said to me: "Did you know that Abraham Lincoln was born in Clark county, near Thatcher's Mill?" "No," said I, "but I have heard it." Mayor ——— continued: "When Hay and Nicholay began writing the history of Mr. Lincoln, some one wrote to Mat. ———, in their interest, asking him (———) to write what he knew concerning Mr. Lincoln's birth-place. ——— came to me and told me that Mr. Lincoln was

born near Thatcher's Mill, out of wedlock, and
said: " *Shall I tell what I know?* " " No," said
I, " keep it to yourself. You might get into
trouble." ———— did not write what he knew
in response to the inquiries of Hay and
Nicholay.

Mayor John —. ———— repeated the above
statement to me before Mr. John ————
————, formerly editor of the Winchester
Sun (Republican newspaper), and candidate
for Congress against W. M. ———— in the
election to fill the unexpired term in Congress
of Hon. Marcus ——, deceased, — —, 1894.

Judge W. M. ————, M. C., met me
before the Citizens' Bank of Winchester, and
I said to him: " Judge, I suppose that you—
like all old residents of Clark—have heard that
Mr. Lincoln was born near Thatcher's Mill,

and born out of wedlock?" "Oh, yes," replied Judge ———; "Senator —— told me all about it." " Will you give me your written statement to that effect?" said I. " Oh, yes; at any *time*," he said, very pleasantly.

In a few weeks after this meeting I went to him after his written statement. He put me off on one trifling pretext or another, until I followed him up and said to him: "Judge ———, didn't you tell me that Senator —— told you that Mr. Lincoln was born out of wedlock, near Thatcher's Mill?" "Yes," said Judge ———; " I told you that; but, after thinking about the matter, I do not want to be in it."

Colonel R. N. ——, James ———, son of Chief-Justice ———, and many others— as responsible as they—confirmed the statements made in the three affidavits of Dr. H. ——, William ——, and Daniel ——. I think I could get a thousand affidavits in Kentucky to prove the statements in those I now possess.

LUCINDA BOYD.

STATE OF KENTUCKY, } *sct.:*
  FAYETTE COUNTY. }

Subscribed and sworn to before me by Lucinda Boyd, this September 25, 1895.

[SEAL.]   CLAUDE CHINN,

Clerk Fayette County Court, Kentucky.

———

Exact copy of affidavit of Judge B. J. ——, who for sixteen years was Chief Justice of Kentucky:

I am ninety years old. I was Judge of

the Court of Appeals of Kentucky for sixteen
years, and then retired on account of ad-
vancing years.

I was graduated from Transylvania Uni-
versity, Kentucky, in 1825. I read law with
John ——, Chief Justice of Kentucky; ob-
tained license to practice law in 1827. My
legal and professional career has extended over
a period of sixty years. In all that time I have
never heard, among my legal friends (and I
know nearly all the lawyers, old and young,
in the State) the fact of Abraham Lincoln's
illegitimacy disputed.

The late Colonel ——, a prominent man
in the Kentucky Legislature, said to me: "I
heard —— ——, then a resident of Harrods-
burg, Ky., say that he had married Nancy
Hornback, Hanks, or Sparrow in Washington

county, Ky., to Thomas Lincoln, and that at the time of the marriage of the said Nancy Hornback, Hanks, or Sparrow and Thomas Lincoln that Nancy's son Abraham (afterwards called Lincoln) was a boy large enough to run around."

A lady, who said her maiden name was Hanks* and place of residence Massachusetts (I think), came to me last summer and asked me if I had not heard the Hankses, of Montgomery, say that Abraham Lincoln's mother was named Hanks. I told her no, that I never had, but had always heard that her name was Hornback. She is the only one I ever heard express a doubt of Abraham Lincoln's illegitimacy.

B. J. —   —,

Ex-Chief Justice of Kentucky.

———

* Mrs. Tarball who wrote the history of Mr. Lincoln in McClure's Magazine.

I am willing to make oath to the foregoing statement before any officer authorized to administer oaths.

B. J. ———.

Subscribed to and sworn to before me by B. J. ———, this 24th day of January, 1896.

[SEAL.] DOUGLAS DAY,

Notary Public.

———

In Herndon's book, now almost out of print, entitled "A History of Abraham Lincoln," this passage is to be found:

(Mr. Herndon was the law partner of Mr. Lincoln in Springfield, Ill.)

"We were driving together one day, and Mr. Lincoln said to me: 'God bless my mother—all I am I owe to her—she was

illegitimate, but the best *blood of Virginia
ran in her veins.'*"

From telling that truth Mr. Herndon's
book was scorned and tabooed.

———

MT. STERLING, KY., January 23, 1896.
To Whom It May Concern:

I am thirty-nine years old, have been an
attorney at law since 1881, engaged in the
practice of law at Mt. Sterling; have been
Prosecuting Attorney for Montgomery
county, Ky., and am now Special Judge of
Montgomery Circuit Court. Have been
several years associated in the same office with
Ex-Chief Justice B. J. ————, and have known
him well since 1880. He was for sixteen years
Judge of the Kentucky Court of Appeals, and,

until now, or very recently, he has been in active practice of the law, and is now in the full possession of all his faculties, and wonderfully and remarkably well preserved, both in mind and body. He was, until the last few months, president of the Exchange Bank of Mt. Sterling, Ky., which is in good condition, this 23d of January, 1896.

H. M. ——————.

Special Judge Montgomery Circuit Court.

———

I regard Judge B. J. —— as a man of sound mind, and that he is of remarkable vigor, both mentally and physically, for a man of his years.

H. P. ——————.

Cashier Exchange Bank.

The affiant, Thomas ——, states that he
was born May 11, 1802, in Bourbon county,
Ky., near North Middleton, and near
Thatcher's Mill, which is on the line which
separates Clark county from Bourbon county,
in the said State aforesaid.

He further states that he has heard responsible persons say, and that it was the cur-
rent and generally accepted belief, and familiar
to him ever since boyhood, that a certain male
child named Abraham, and called Abraham
Lincoln, was born near said Thatcher's Mill,
in Bourbon county, and that he was the child
of Nancy Hanks, Hornback, or Sparrow, and a
young man who came from Virginia. Many
persons have told me that they saw the said
Nancy and Thomas Lincoln leave Thatcher's
Mill with the said child Abraham sitting be-

tween them, and they were said to be start-
ing for another county in Kentucky to get
married and reside.

Witness my mark, this October 7, 1895.

His
THOMAS (X) ————.
Witness: Mark.

H. G. BRATTON.

JOHN I. FISHER.

Subscribed and sworn to by Thomas
————, October 7, 1895, in the presence of
H. G. Bratton and John I. Fisher.

[SEAL.]   ED. P. BEAN, JR.,

Notary Public.

————

Affidavit of the late Hubbard ————, M. D.:

I have heard from reliable sources ever

since I was a boy that Abraham (afterwards
called Abraham Lincoln) was born at
Thatcher's Mill, out of wedlock, and that he
was the son of Nancy Hanks, Hornback, or
Sparrow, who lived with other women, near
Thatcher's Mill, and of a young man from
Virginia. I have seen persons, after I was
grown, who had seen Thomas Lincoln and
Nancy, the aforesaid, leave Thatcher's Mill
with Abraham sitting between them, on their
way to be married elsewhere.

Abraham Inlow and one Roberts paid
Thomas Lincoln to marry the aforesaid
Nancy, because of her poverty and youth, and
their pity for Nancy on account of them. I
am eighty-three years old. I have been a
practicing physician in Winchester and Clark
county, Ky., and in other places for more

than 50 (fifty) years, and have heard the story a hundred times.

HUBBARD ————, M. D.

Subscribed to and sworn to before me, this the 24th day of September, 1895.

F. B. HODGKINS,

Examiner for Clark County, Ky.

————

Affidavit of William ————:

William ————, born in Winchester sixty-nine years ago of parents who had lived there since their youth, said to me, in the presence of witnesses:

" Daniel Thatcher, owner of Thatcher's Mill, built about the year 1800, said to me in ———— presence Abraham Lincoln (so

called) was born near Thatcher's Mill, not in
the stone house, as many suppose, but in a log
cabin long since destroyed. His mother's
name was Nancy Hanks, Hornback, or Sparrow, I don't know which, and his father was a
young man from the State of Virginia.

Mat. ———, who lived there (at Thatcher's
Mill), also said: " Yes; I have letters to prove
this statement, but I intend to burn them."
Hundreds of persons now alive in Clark
county, Ky., remember to have heard responsible persons say that they had seen
Thomas Lincoln and Nancy Hanks, Hornback, or Sparrow, leave Thatcher's Mill with
Abraham between them on their way to be
married elsewhere.

Abraham Inlow, Portuguese Miller, of
Thatcher's Mill, felt very sorry for young

Nancy Hanks, Hornback, or Sparrow, who lived in the cabin aforesaid, and especially for Nancy and her child Abraham, who was named for him (Abraham Inlow), and he and a man by the name of Roberts paid Thomas Lincoln, stonemason of Clark (county), and native of Virginia, to marry Nancy. He consented, and they (Nancy the aforesaid and Thomas Lincoln) left Thatcher's Mill with *Abraham between them,* to be married elsewhere.

WILLIAM ————————.

Subscribed and sworn to before me, the 24th day of September, 1895.

J. M. HODGKIN,
Notary Public.

————

My name is Daniel ——. I was born in 1833, the 13th day of August, near and in sight of Thatcher's Mill, in Bourbon county, near the line between Clark and Bourbon counties, Ky. When Abraham Lincoln made the race for President of the United States I heard that Abraham Lincoln was born near Thatcher's Mill, out of wedlock. During and at the time of Mr. Lincoln's race for the presidency I heard the above-named facts.

DANIEL ————.

Subscribed and sworn to before me by Daniel ————, this September 24, 1895.

G. F. BURNER,
Ex. C. C. Ky.
(Resident of Winchester, Ky.)

————

MT. STERLING, KY., January 23, 1896.
My Dear Madam:

I have known Mr. Abraham Lincoln quite

sixty years by tradition. About thirty years or more I knew him personally.

He was born near Thatcher's Mill, in the county of Bourbon, and State of Kentucky. His mother's name was Nancy Hornback. His father's name was Abraham Inlow. Mr. A. Lincoln was born out of wedlock. This is in brief the tradition of my father and mother, and of the entire Inlow family for seventy years at least. His father was my mother's uncle, and my grandfather's brother. As to his birth, the above are the traditional facts in the family—and all the early settlers of Bourbon county at the time of his birth.

Very truly, etc.,

M. M. — ‑‑‑‑‑‑.

Ex-Judge.

www.ingramcontent.com/pod-product-compliance
Lightning Source LLC
Chambersburg PA
CBHW021412090426
42742CB00009B/1117

9 783337 778293